GROUNDBREAKERS

John C. Frémont

Karen Price Hossell

Heinemann Library
Chicago, Illinois

Customer Service 888-454-2279

Visit our website at www.heinemannlibrary.com

Page layout and maps by 3 Loop 9, Los Angeles, CA.
Photo research by Amor Montes de Oca
Printed and bount in the United States by Lake Book Manufacturing, Inc.

07 06 05 04 03
10 9 8 7 6 5 4 3 2 1

Library of Congress Cataloging-in-Publication Data
Price Hossell, Karen, 1957–
    John C. Frémont / Karen Price Hossell.
       p. cm. – (Groundbreakers)
    Summary: Gives an account of the life of John C. Frémont, a surveyor, mapmaker, and
explorer who traveled through the western United States in the middle of the
nineteenth century.
    Includes bibliographical references and index.
      ISBN 1-4034-0244-2 (library binding-hardcover) – ISBN 1-4034-0480-1 (pbk.)
      1. Frémont, John Charles, 1813-1890–Juvenile literature. 2. Explorers—United States
--Biography—Juvenile literature. 3. Explorers—West (U.S.)—Biography—Juvenile literature.
4. West (U.S.)—Discovery and exploration—Juvenile literature. 5. Generals—United States
--Juvenile literature. 7. United States—Territorial expansion—Juvenile literature.
[1. Frémont, John Charles, 1813-1890. 2. Explorers. 3. West (U.S.)—Discovery and
exploration.]   I. Title. II. Series.
E415.9.F8P74 2002
973.6'092—dc21
    [B]
                                                                    2002008343

Acknowledgments
The author and publishers are grateful to the following for permission to reproduce copyright material:
pp. 4, 8, 9, 11, 13, 14, 15, 26, 30, 32, 38, 39 The Granger Collection, New York; pp. 5, 6, 10, 12, 16,
17, 18, 22, 25, 27, 28, 31, 40 North Wind Picture Archives; p. 7 Michael Durham; p. 19 Library of
Congress; p. 20 Hulton Archive/Getty Images; p. 21 David Muench/Corbis; p. 23 Robert
Holmes/Corbis; pp. 24, 29, 33, 37 Corbis; pp. 34, 35 David J. & Janice L. Frent Collection/Corbis; p. 36
Bettmann/Corbis; p. 41 Jeff Greenberg/Visuals Unlimited

Cover photograph by The Granger Collection, New York

Some words are shown in bold, **like this.** You can find out
what they mean by looking in the glossary.

Contents

Who Was John Charles Frémont?

John Charles Frémont was a **surveyor,** mapmaker, and explorer who traveled through the western United States in the middle of the nineteenth century. While Frémont's nickname was "The Pathfinder," most historians agree that he was really a pathmarker. Instead of finding paths, he followed the paths that others, such as Native Americans, fur trappers, and hunters, had made before him. What sets Frémont apart from those pathfinders is that he was the first to put those paths and trails on a map.

Explorer

Frémont led several **expeditions** that are important because the information that was gathered on the expeditions was used to make maps. The maps were among the first to be made of certain regions in the American West. One map was used by **pioneers** as they traveled across the Oregon Trail. Other maps, along with published reports of the expeditions, gave the American public its first glimpses of the Great Salt Lake and the Great Basin.

Politician

Frémont was also involved in politics. Though very popular as an explorer, he was not as popular as a politician. He was involved in a political **controversy** in California, just before it became a state.

John C. Frémont lived a life of adventure and led several scientific expeditions throughout the American West. The information he and his men gathered on the expeditions was used to make some of the first maps of these western regions.

In 1842, Frémont climbed what he thought was the highest mountain in the Rocky Mountain range and planted a flag at its summit. Today the mountain is called Frémont's Peak.

For a short time, he was governor of California, and he was one of its first senators. Later, he ran for president, although he lost the election to James Buchanan. During the Civil War, President Abraham Lincoln made Frémont a general in the Union Army, only to strip him of the rank after more controversy. Later, Frémont was the governor of the **territory** of Arizona.

Businessman

Frémont was also a businessman. He bought land in California just before gold was discovered there in 1848. Several gold mines were found on his land, and he made millions of dollars from them. But Frémont proved to be a poor businessman, and after several bad business decisions, he lost all of his money.

John Charles Frémont was a popular character throughout his life. Reports of his adventures fascinated the public. He was as comfortable in the social circles of Washington, D.C., as he was riding on horseback across the deserts and plains of the West. He made friends not only with inventors, scientists, and senators, but also with mountain men such as Kit Carson.

John Charles Frémon was born on January 21, 1813, in Savannah, Georgia. He added the "t" to the end of his name later, so that it would sound more American. His father, Charles, was born in France but left that country in about 1799, ending up in Norfolk, Virginia. For most of his adult life, Charles Frémon taught French. Sometimes he taught in schools, and sometimes he was a private **tutor.** One of the students he taught privately was Mrs. Anne Pryor. The two fell in love and ran away together. After Mrs. Pryor's husband died, Charles and Anne married. In 1813, John was born. For much of his childhood, John and his family moved around, traveling from Savannah to Nashville, Tennessee, and then to Norfolk. During those years, his mother gave birth to another son and a daughter.

Boyhood in Charleston

In about 1818, when John was 5 years old, Charles Frémon died. Mrs. Frémon then moved her family to Charleston, South Carolina. John enjoyed Charleston. As a young boy, he liked to go to the harbor and watch ships sail away. He imagined the adventures the people on board the ships would have at foreign ports. John also liked sailing, fishing, and hunting, and he had many friends.

Charleston was founded in 1670 and named after King Charles II of England. Its deep natural harbor helped to make it an important port city.

Frémont's education

John did so well in school that when he was fourteen years old, a friend of the family paid for him to go to a private school run by Dr. Charles Robinson. The school prepared young men to enter Charleston College. At the school, John learned Latin, Greek, and mathematics. He was so bright that Dr. Robinson decided John was ready to enter Charleston College at the age of sixteen.

John did very well at college for a while, and he especially enjoyed studying mathematics and science.

For thousands of years, people like Frémont have observed the movements of the stars and planets to aid in navigation.

The college had a rule that all students had to spend at least seven hours a day on campus, except for Saturdays and Sundays. At first John followed the rule. But then he started spending more and more time away from school, going sailing and fishing with friends.

Expelled

The head of the college warned John that if he did not start attending classes regularly, he would be **expelled.** John didn't listen. On February 5, 1831, just three months before he was to graduate, the college told him he must leave.

While his family and teachers were upset that John had been expelled from Charleston College, John did not seem to care. He said that he finally felt free. For a while, he taught at a local school. When he wasn't teaching, hunting, fishing, or sailing, John studied **astronomy.** He was fascinated by the science of the stars.

Frémont and Poinsett

While John was still attending Charleston College, he met Joel Roberts Poinsett. Poinsett knew some of the teachers at the college. He often asked the teachers and the **headmaster** whether there were any bright young men there he could help. The people at the school told Poinsett about John.

When he met John, Poinsett was impressed by his intelligence and enthusiasm. He invited the young man to the weekly breakfasts he held for people in society. There, John met many wealthy, interesting people who had traveled a great deal. At the breakfasts, he listened to their stories and to Poinsett as he talked. Poinsett had formerly served as the American Minister to Mexico. He had also traveled to many other countries. These stories of adventure made John eager to see the world.

JOEL ROBERTS POINSETT

Poinsett was one of the most well-traveled Americans of his time. He went to school in the United States, England, and Scotland, studying medicine and law. President James Madison sent Poinsett to South America in 1810, and he was later appointed American Minister to Mexico, representing American interests in that country. Poinsett was always interested in botany—the study of plants—and he collected plants as he traveled and sent them to various gardens in the United States. One plant he collected was a red flower from Mexico. Some Americans had seen the plant before, but Poinsett grew many of them in South Carolina and gave them to friends as gifts, helping to make them popular. The plant soon was named after Poinsett, and today many people decorate with the poinsettia during the winter holidays.

Teaching aboard the *Natchez*

With Poinsett's help, John got a job teaching mathematics on a navy ship, the *Natchez*. Today, those who join the U.S. Navy often go to a Naval Academy to study, but in the 1800s, there was no such school. Instead, sailors took classes on board ship as they sailed.

As the ship traveled, John had a chance to see ports in South America and other places. He loved traveling, but he didn't like teaching as much as he thought he would. Still, when his

Starting in 1833, when he was only twenty years old, Frémont taught mathematics aboard a naval ship similar to this one.

time aboard the *Natchez* ended, John decided to apply to become a full-time mathematics professor in the Navy. By that time, the leaders of Charleston College had decided to give John his college degree.

Frémont joins the Topographical Corps

John studied every day for a month for the test he had to take to become a professor. He passed the test but then changed his mind about being a professor. Again with Poinsett's help, John had been given another opportunity, one he preferred. He was to join a branch of the Army called the United States **Topographical** Corps and help them **survey** a route for a railroad.

Frémont's job with the United States **Topographical** Corps was to help find a route for a railroad. The job took him to the mountains of North Carolina and Tennessee.

Surveying

Frémont loved working outside, and he liked working with **surveying** equipment. He was able to use his skills in math and science at the job. He did so well that after the job was finished his boss, Captain Williams, asked Frémont to help him on another job. This time, the men went to the mountains of Georgia. The government was moving the Cherokee Indians who lived on the land and wanted a complete survey of the area.

As Frémont worked in Georgia, he began to realize what he wanted to do with his life. He wanted to live and work outside, among Native Americans, if he could.

Opportunity in the West

The job in Georgia lasted from 1836 to 1837. Frémont went back to Charleston when his work was finished. By that time, Poinsett had been appointed Secretary of War under President Van Buren. The U.S. government wanted to explore more of the western part of the United States. The land between the upper Mississippi River and the upper Missouri River in particular needed to be explored.

Throughout the nineteenth century, goverment surveyors were kept busy mapping the West. They often had to travel across difficult terrain.

The Cherokee Indians lived in the mountains of North Carolina, Tennessee, and Georgia, until they were forced off their lands by the U.S. government.

The only people who really knew their way around the region were fur trappers, and they didn't know anything about surveying and mapping. Poinsett knew someone who did, though—his young friend, John Frémont. Frémont, he knew, had already been on two surveying **expeditions.** Poinsett thought Frémont would be a good man to do the survey.

With Poinsett's help, Frémont became a second **lieutenant** in the U.S. Topographical Corps in 1838. Then he set off for his trip west. Frémont was excited about his new job. He had always wanted to see the wide open spaces he'd heard about in the West, and he wanted to see how western Native Americans lived.

THE TRAIL OF TEARS

In 1836 and 1837, the United States government sent Frémont to survey the western part of Georgia. The government was planning to force the Cherokee people off the land they had lived on for about 1,000 years. One reason the government wanted the land was that gold was discovered there. The removal was the result of the "Indian Removal Act" passed by Congress in 1830. Many Americans disagreed with the Act and thought the Cherokee should be allowed to keep their land, but Congress passed the Act and President Andrew Jackson signed it into law. In 1838, the government began to move the Cherokee 1,000 miles (1,600 kilometers) away to Oklahoma. They had to travel by foot. The route they took on their journey is often called "The Trail of Tears." About 15,000 Cherokee were moved, and 4,000 died on the long journey.

Frémont and Nicollet

YOU CAN FOLLOW FRÉMONT'S EXPEDITION ON THE MAP ON PAGES 42–43.

The man in charge of the **surveying expedition** was Joseph Nicolas Nicollet. He was a respected scientist, and like Frémont's father, he was French. From Nicollet and the others on the trip, Frémont learned many things that would help him on his future expeditions. Their guide taught Frémont how to pack a mule so the pack wouldn't fall off, even if the mule was walking down a steep hill. He also learned how to pitch a tent and how to cook food over a campfire.

From Nicollet, Frémont learned about the science of surveying and about botany, the study of plants. He also learned how to use the stars to determine his location and how to study the land so he could make good maps.

Learning from the Sioux

Frémont and Nicollet worked together on two expeditions. In 1838, they traveled up the Minnesota River through lands inhabited by the Sioux. As they traveled through the land between the upper Mississippi and Missouri Rivers, the surveying team often met Native Americans. Many of the people Frémont met as he worked were Sioux. He learned how they lived and how to talk to them. Frémont also saw

*French-Canadian **voyageurs** explored Canada and the northern United States, trapping and trading furs. They had a reputation for being hardy, resourceful travelers.*

huge herds of bison and watched the Sioux as they hunted them and dried the meat in strips. (Although they look like other types of buffalo, the American buffalo is actually a separate species: bison.) During the trip Frémont carefully drew maps of the locations they studied. He was becoming an explorer.

The expedition stopped during the winter of 1838, then resumed in 1839. During this expedition, Nicollet, Frémont, and the other explorers traveled through present-day North and South Dakota.

In Frémont's words:

One night, Nicollet invited some members of the Sioux tribe to have dinner at the surveyors' camp. Frémont describes the meal this way:

"The chiefs sat around in a large circle on buffalo robes or blankets, each provided with a deep soup plate and a spoon of tin. . . . When all was ready the feast began. With the first mouthful each Indian silently laid down his spoon, and each looked at the other. After a pause of bewilderment the interpreter succeeded in having the situation understood. Mr. Nicollet had put among our provisions some Swiss cheese, and to give flavor to the soup a liberal portion of this had been put into the kettles. Until this strange flavor was accounted for the Indians though they were being poisoned."

At the beginning of the nineteenth century, millions of bison roamed the American plains. As the West was settled by Americans from the East, though, their numbers fell. By the end of the century so many bison had been killed that they were almost extinct.

The Bentons

When the **expedition** was finished, Nicollet and Frémont went to Washington, D.C. There, they were invited to many parties and dinners. After a few weeks of rest, they began to make maps, using the information they had gathered on their trip.

Thomas Hart Benton

At one social gathering Frémont met a senator from Missouri named Thomas Hart Benton. Benton was known for his eagerness to settle the land beyond the Missouri River. He believed that it was the **manifest destiny** of the United States to make the West a part of the United States. He and Frémont

Senator Thomas Hart Benton was a great speaker who encouraged Americans to settle the West.

became good friends, and Frémont spent a lot of time at Benton's home. He and Senator Benton talked about the West and how someone should **survey** and make maps of the area. Frémont, of course, thought he would be the perfect person for the job.

Jessie Benton

Frémont found something else to interest him at Benton's home—Benton's daughter Jessie. She was fifteen years old when Frémont met her, and she was beautiful, funny, and intelligent. The two fell in love and became engaged. Mr. and Mrs. Benton, however, were not happy about the relationship. They thought Jessie was too young to think about marriage. Besides, Frémont was just an army man. They wanted their daughter to marry someone with a more important job, someone who made more money. The Bentons told the young couple to stay away from each other. Then Mrs. Benton went to see Mrs. Poinsett, the wife of Frémont's old friend Joel Poinsett. After their meeting, Frémont was suddenly given orders to begin another surveying job. Before Frémont left, Senator Benton said that if the two still wanted to get married when Frémont returned, he would allow it.

Frémont and Jessie marry

Frémont traveled to the Iowa **territory** to survey the Des Moines River. When he returned several months later, he and Jessie still wanted to marry. They waited a while for the senator to give his approval, but they soon got tired of waiting. On October 19, 1841, they **eloped** with the help of a friend. It took Senator Benton a while to accept the marriage between his daughter and Frémont. Once he did, he allowed Frémont to move into his house.

Jessie Ann Benton received a better education than most young women at that time. She was fluent in French and Spanish and sometimes helped her father by translating Spanigh government documents.

WHAT IS MANIFEST DESTINY?

Beginning in the 1840s, many people wanted the United States to expand into Texas, Oregon, and Mexico. They said it was the country's "manifest destiny" to do so. Manifest destiny was based on the idea that it was God's will that the country grow to include the entire continent. The concept led to the attempt to take over Mexico, which was larger than it is now. That started the Mexican-American War, which lasted from 1846 to 1848. When the war ended, the United States had won a huge area southwest of the United States. In return, the United States agreed to give Mexico five million dollars.

Frémont Leads His First Expedition

In the early 1840s, people were beginning to travel to the West to settle. Many went to the Columbia River region of Oregon. The path they traveled on their long journey was called the Oregon Trail. At one point, the Trail went through a place in the Rocky Mountains called South Pass. Trappers and mountain men had known for years that this pass was the best way to get through the Rockies, and they often were hired as guides by groups of settlers.

In Frémont's words:

Just before he led his first **expedition**, Frémont realized that his purpose in life was to explore new lands. He wrote that his ideal job

". . . would be [to] travel over a part of the world which remained new—the opening up of unknown lands; the making unknown countries known; and the study without books—the learning at first hand from nature itself; the drinking first at her unknown springs."

About one in ten people who traveled on the Oregon Trail died along the way. Some people walked the entire 2,000-mile (3,200-kilometer) trail barefoot.

The trappers and mountain men, though, did not know how to make maps. The U.S. government decided that the **Topographical** Corps should map the South Pass and nearby areas, including the Wind River Mountains, which were part of Rocky Mountain range. The government also wanted to scout locations to put forts to protect travelers from Native Americans who sometimes attacked. Nicollet was their first choice for the job, but he had become ill and could not go. With Benton's help, Frémont was selected to lead the **surveying** and mapping expedition.

Preparing for the expedition

Frémont selected several men who were experienced in traveling through the West to go with him. The men bought supplies and packed them into eight mule carts. They also bought four oxen to help carry supplies and pull carts. Besides these experienced mountain men and **voyageurs,** Frémont brought along a German **cartographer** named Charles Preuss and young Randolph Benton, Jessie's brother. Then Frémont hired one more man, an experienced guide named Kit Carson.

CHARLES PREUSS

The cartographer Charles Preuss came to the United States from Germany in 1834. At the time, the U.S. government was doing a survey of the country's coastline, and Preuss spent several years working on that project. He quit in 1839 to work for a mining company, but that job didn't work out. Because he had a family to support, Preuss desperately needed work, so he joined Frémont's first expedition. His diaries provide an important record of the day-to-day life of the expedition. As he traveled through the West, Preuss became homesick not only for his family but also for a comfortable bed and good food. Still, he seemed to enjoy doing his job, and when his maps were published they were considered to be among the best available. Preuss went on Frémont's first and second expeditions but retired from exploring at the age of fifty.

Exploring the South Pass

YOU CAN FOLLOW FRÉMONT'S EXPEDITION ON THE MAP ON PAGES 42–43.

Frémont and his men set off from St. Louis, Missouri, on about May 22, 1842. The supply-filled carts traveled only 24 miles (39 kilometers) a day. The men stopped about an hour before dark to set up camp. They went to sleep at about 9:00 P.M. and woke up at 4:30 A.M. By 6:30 they were traveling. Frémont described plants, streams, hills, mountains, and rivers in his journal. He also used special instruments to make **astronomical** observations that could be used later to make maps. Preuss drew pictures of many geographical features so they could be included on the maps.

In Kit Carson's words:

"I was with Frémont from 1842 to 1847. The hardships through which we passed, I find it impossible to describe, and the credit which he deserves I am incapable to do him justice in writing. . . . I can never forget his treatment of me while in his employ and how cheerfully he suffered with his men when undergoing the severest of hardships."

The travelers followed the Kansas River to the Platte River, which led them to the Rockies. On August 8, 1842, they reached the South Pass, which is in present-day Wyoming. Then they traveled farther west, to the Wind River Mountains.

Frémont's descriptions of Kit Carson in his published reports made him a famous national figure. Carson was a trapper, soldier, Indian scout, and guide.

Many artists drew their own versions of Frémont planting the flag, and they did not always get the details right. The flag Frémont actually used looked slightly different.

Frémont plants a flag

Before turning back, Frémont calculated which mountain was the highest. With five other men, he climbed the mountain on August 15, 1842. At the top, Frémont planted a flag. On the flag were thirteen stripes. In one corner was a blue eagle against a white field. The eagle held a peace pipe and blue stars in his talons. The mountain is now called Frémont's Peak, but at 13,730 feet (4,185 meters), it is not actually the highest mountain in the Rockies.

A popular report

In the fall and winter of 1842 and 1843, Frémont wrote a report of his journey, with Jessie's help. Preuss made a set of maps to go with the report. Copies of the report were sold to the public. Frémont's words and Preuss's maps made for popular reading, and Frémont soon became well known throughout the United States. Kit Carson became a famous figure as well. Frémont's descriptions of Carson's adventures before and during the **expedition** fascinated his readers.

STUDYING THE SKY

Frémont used special tools such as telescopes, sextants, chronometers, compasses, barometers, and thermometers to determine his location as he traveled. One way he calculated his location was by finding **constellations** and planets and recording them in his journal. When he got home, he consulted a book written by astronomers to find out where those objects were in the sky on the day he located them. With that information, he could find his **latitude** and **longitude** on the day he saw the objects on his expedition. He used that information to make maps.

The Expedition of 1843

YOU CAN FOLLOW FRÉMONT'S EXPEDITION ON THE MAP ON PAGES 42–43.

In 1843, the **Topographical** Corps sent Frémont on another **expedition.** Earlier, an explorer named Charles Wilkes had **surveyed** the area along the Pacific coast in northern California. Frémont was to end his journey where it met up with Wilkes's. Charles Preuss and Kit Carson would go along on this journey, too. Altogether, the expedition included 39 men. Most were hardy **voyageurs,** but there were also two Delaware Indian guides. The expedition also had thirteen carts, many horses and mules, and a cannon.

MEDALS AND HONORS

Frémont received several medals and other honors for his expeditions. Among them is a gold sword from he state of California, given to honor his work there and in Oregon. He also received a medal from the Royal Geographic Society in London, England.

The Great Salt Lake

The men traveled up the Snake River to the Columbia River. There, the party divided into two. One group went to Fort Hall, and Frémont led another group south to the Great Salt Lake. This large body of salt water is in present-day Utah. Frémont took a rubber boat out onto the lake and collected water. When he got back to camp, he boiled the water until all that was left was salt. He was impressed that 5 gallons (19 liters) of water from the lake boiled down to 14 pints (6.6 liters) of salt.

*The Missouri River runs through Westport Landing in Kansas City. In the 1800s this made it a popular starting point for groups of **pioneers** heading west.*

The Great Salt Lake, which is in Utah, covers about 2,100 square miles (5,438 square kilometers). Its average depth is 13 feet (4 meters).

A rough journey ahead

After Frémont's party left the lake, they met up with the group at Fort Hall. There, Frémont called his men together and told them that the next part of the journey would not be easy. If anyone wanted to leave, he said, they could. Eleven men rode away.

The Great Basin

Frémont and the remaining expedition members continued west to the point where the Snake, Walla Walla, Columbia, and Yakima rivers meet to form the lower Columbia River. Next, they searched the Great Basin area for a river that flowed from the Rockies to the Pacific. The Great Basin includes parts of Utah, Nevada, and New Mexico, about 190,000 square miles (492,000 square kilometers) in all. For many years, people had said that a river, called the Buenaventura, flowed from the Rocky Mountains into the Pacific. Frémont searched and searched for such a river and finally decided that it did not exist.

Climbing the Sierra Nevada

Instead of turning eastward toward home, Frémont decided that he wanted to see California. To do that, the men would have to cross the Sierra Nevada. Snow had already begun to fall before the travelers began to accend the high peaks. On January 19, 1844, the expedition party started the steep climb up the mountains.

Crossing into California

You can follow Frémont's expedition on the map on pages 42–43.

Historians agree that Frémont's decision to cross the Sierra Nevada in January 1844 was not a good one. The snow was already at least three feet (one meter) deep when the men urged their horses up the trail. Frémont had already achieved the goal of the **expedition,** so he could have changed his mind and decided to turn back. Instead, he pressed on.

Snow and more snow

The snow on the mountains was hard-packed and had an icy surface. When the horses and mules stepped into the snow, they sometimes cut their legs on the hard ice. Riders took turns leading the expedition, packing down the snow for those who came behind. On January 29, they had to leave the cannon behind. By February 4, some of the horses refused to move. Some were pushed or pulled, and others died on the trail. The travelers began to dump supplies to save weight. At the crest of the mountain range, the snow was 5 feet (1.5 meters) deep. The reflection of the sun on the snow was so bright that the men had to wear black handkerchiefs over their eyes. Because the grass was hidden under feet of snow, the animals began to starve. They chewed on one another's tails and on the leather saddles.

The Sierra Nevada range separates Nevada and California. Frémont and his men crossed the range in winter, enduring harsh conditions before ending up in the Sacramento Valley.

Sutter's Fort is now a state park in Sacramento, California.

Into California

On February 20, 1844, the party finally reached the summit of the mountain range. They stopped and gazed at the beautiful Sacramento Valley below. Never had they seen such a welcome sight as the green valley. They began their descent, and on March 6 they reached the valley. About 30 horses and mules had died on the journey, but all of the men survived.

The group went to Sutter's Fort in California. There, they had a **blacksmith** make new shoes for their horses and mules, and they bought new saddles and bridles. They also bought fresh horses, as well as cows to kill and eat along the way. In all, they had about 130 horses and mules and 30 head of cattle. Two days later, they set off on their return trip. At first they traveled south to a pass they had heard about. Then they went into Colorado, where one man was killed by Native Americans when he went back to help a sick mule. On July 1, 1844, the exhausted men finally ended their journey.

Planning a Third Expedition

YOU CAN FOLLOW FRÉMONT'S EXPEDITION ON THE MAP ON PAGES 42–43.

Back in Washington, D.C., Frémont and Jessie worked on the report of Frémont's **expedition.** They completed the 300-page report in February 1845. Many people were eager to read the report, so more than 10,000 copies were printed. Seven maps went along with the report. The maps were very helpful to anyone traveling on the Oregon Trail. They included details such as distances between one place and another, the best places to cross rivers, the best grazing areas, and which Native American tribes lived where.

Into the Rockies again

As soon as the report was finished, Frémont began to plan his third expedition to the West. The army wanted him to explore the Rockies again. He was told to find a northern route from California to Oregon, through the Cascade Mountains in northern California. He was also instructed to find a route to southern California through the Sierra Nevada range and to continue to explore the Great Salt Lake.

Threats of war

The army had a reason for being so interested in finding good trails to California. At that time, most of California was claimed by Mexico,

MAP OF OREGON AND UPPER CALIFORNIA
From the Surveys of
JOHN CHARLES FRÉMONT
And other Authorities
DRAWN BY CHARLES PREUSS
Under the Order of the
SENATE OF THE UNITED STATES
Washington City 1848.
Scale 1:3000000

This map is the one Preuss made after the second expedition. His maps are highly valued by modern collectors.

except for northern California, which was mainly occupied by British traders. The U.S. government expected Great Britain to start fighting with the United States over possession of the land. The government also expected trouble with Mexico. The United States had just **annexed** Texas, which had already been claimed by Mexico. The U.S. government had sent someone to Mexico to offer to pay for Texas, but the Mexican government wanted the land, not money. A war between Mexico and the United States over Texas seemed almost sure to happen.

On to California

Frémont's third expedition began in August 1845. This time, Charles Preuss did not go along because his wife wanted him to stay home for a while. There were 60 men on this expedition, more than on any of the others. Also, this time the men carried better firearms than the men did in past expeditions.

The expedition blazed a trail through Nevada. Then Frémont decided that the best way to fulfill the goals of the expedition would be to split the party into two groups. That way, the men could cover more ground. Every few weeks, the two groups would meet and report their findings.

California became a province of Mexico in 1822, after Mexico gained its independence from Spain. A Mexican flag hangs in Mission San Juan Capistrano in California, showing the area's Mexican heritage.

Frémont Takes a Stand

You can follow Frémont's expedition on the map on pages 42–43.

While Frémont and his group of men were exploring California, a Mexican leader told them to leave at once. Frémont refused, even though he was far from the places he had been told to explore. Frémont then climbed a mountain called Hawk's Peak, where he and his men built a fort and raised the American flag in a show of defiance. As they worked, they could see an army of Mexicans gathering below them. Frémont and his men stayed on the mountain for three days, then escaped down the other side and went to the Cascade Mountains in Oregon. One night a messenger from the U.S. Marines named Gillespie came to Oregon looking for Frémont. No one is certain exactly what message Frémont received, but after reading it he decided to take action.

Ready to fight

Frémont gathered his men and, with Gillespie, returned to California, prepared to fight the Mexicans there. Gillespie had told him that the United States and Mexico would soon be at war. Frémont guessed that many Californians would go to Mexico to join the fighting. He also thought—as did many Americans—that the British would take the opportunity to occupy all of California. Frémont knew that President Polk wanted to claim California for the United States, so he made plans to take the land from the Mexicans and keep it safe from the British.

*James K. Polk was the 11th president of the United States and a firm believer in **manifest destiny**. During his presidency the United States border first reached all the way to the Pacific Ocean.*

The Republic of California

Frémont met with a group of Americans who had settled in California. Jose Castro, the Mexican leader in California, had told the Americans that they either had to leave or become citizens of Mexico. If they refused, they would be forced to leave California, and all of their property

The modern state flag of California is based on the one flown during the Bear Flag Revolt. The flag makers chose a grizzly bear to symbolize their strength and unyielding resistance.

would be taken from them. The settlers rebelled against Castro by declaring themselves an independent **republic.** To get weapons and ammunition, they attacked and occupied a small Mexican military base at Sonoma. There, they made a flag for their republic. A star, a grizzly bear, and the words "California Republic" were on the white flag.

In the words of Jessie Benton Frémont:

Jessie wrote these words in a letter to Frémont in 1846, while he was in California. In it she tells how one of their children, Lilly, asked Preuss about a story in Frémont's report of an earlier **expedition.** The little girl calls the report a "lepote."

"As for your Report, its popularity astonished even me, your most confirmed and oldest worshipper. Lilly has it read to her (the stories, of course), as a reward for good behavior. She asked Preuss the other day if it was true that he caught ants on his hands and ate them—he was so amazed that he could not answer her, and she said, 'I read it in papa's lepote; it was when you were lost in California.'"

Trouble in California

You can follow Frémont's expedition on the map on pages 42–43.

By June of 1846, Frémont had become more concerned with the political situation in California than with exploration. He gathered an army of 234 men, most of them American settlers. The army called itself the California Battalion. Frémont soon found out that the United States and Mexico were officially at war. He began to use his army to defend California for the United States. The problem was that Frémont had not received official orders to do so. He was acting on his own.

Commodore Stockton

The United States sent battleships to the California coast, but they saw little fighting. The man who was in charge of the ships, though, Commodore Robert F. Stockton, eventually came ashore. He and Frémont worked together to win California. Frémont, Gillespie, Stockton, and their army of men soon controlled much of California.

*In 1847, Robert Stockton proclaimed that California was a **territory** of the United States.*

Brigadier General Kearny

In January 1847, Stephen Watts Kearny came to California. Kearny was brigadier general in charge of the Army of the West. He demanded that Frémont and Stockton turn control of California over to him. Based on past military orders, however, Frémont and Stockton had decided that Stockton was military commander-in-chief and governor of California. They ignored Kearny's orders, and on January 16, Stockton declared that Frémont was now governor.

General Stephen Watts Kearny, who was a veteran of the War of 1812, had Frémont arrested for mutiny and insubordination.

Arrest and court-martial

Kearny was angry that the men would not agree to his authority. After a few months, Kearny ordered Frémont to go with him to Fort Leavenworth, an army outpost on the Missouri River. Of the original 60-person **expedition,** 19 men went back with him. Most of the rest stayed in California. At Fort Leavenworth, Frémont was arrested and charged with **mutiny** and disobeying orders. He was ordered to go immediately to Washington, D.C., to stand trial.

Frémont discovered that many Americans were on his side. Nearly everyone in the military and in government, though, agreed that his actions were illegal. He did help to win California, but he should have waited for official orders instead of acting on his own. At his trial, called a **court-martial,** Frémont was declared guilty. On January 31, 1848, he was forced to leave the army. Later, President Polk said that Frémont could stay in the army, but Frémont decided to resign anyway.

Exploration and Politics

You can follow Frémont's expedition on the map on pages 42–43.

Even after his **court-martial,** Frémont remained popular with the American public. He became even more popular when a set of maps based on his last **expedition** to California was published in 1848. Even though he had not gone along on the expedition, Charles Preuss drew the maps based on information gathered by the **topographer** who did go, Edward M. Orton. The maps were helpful to many people, because in 1848 gold was discovered in California. Thousands of people traveled to California to look for gold. They often used the maps to guide them.

The expedition of 1848

In early 1848, Frémont learned that the U.S. government was looking for **surveyors.** The government was exploring the possibility of building a railroad from the east to the west and wanted to find the best place to lay the tracks in the southern Rockies. Frémont wanted to make the trip, even though he was no longer a member of the U.S. **Topographical** Corps. He spoke to wealthy people he knew to see if they would help pay for his trip. Many agreed to help. On October 21, 1848, Frémont and 33 men set out. They reached Colorado's San Juan Mountains in December and began to search for a location for the railroad to pass through.

The first discovery of Gold at Suter's Mill.

Gold was discovered in California in 1848, and thousands of people came there in 1849 in what is called the California Gold Rush.

The cold and snow encountered by Frémont's expedition took a heavy toll on the men. Weakened by lack of food, they soon became too exhausted to continue.

Soon, though, they had to use all of their energy just to stay alive. The snow in the mountains was sometimes as deep as 30 feet (9 meters). The expedition ran out of supplies. Pack horses and mules collapsed and died from cold and exhaustion. Some men froze to death. Finally, they came out of the mountains and into the **pueblo** of Taos, which is in present-day New Mexico.

Gold!

Frémont went on to California, where he had given a friend money to buy him a ranch. Frémont was not happy about the location of the 43,000 acres (17,400 hectares) of land in Mariposa until gold was discovered there. The gold made Frémont a millionaire. After gold was discovered in California, thousands of Americans moved there in hopes of finding their fortune.

Senator Frémont

In December of 1849, Frémont was elected to the Senate as a Democrat from California. On September 9, 1850, California became a state. Back then, some senators served very short terms. Frémont was one of them—he and the other elected senator from California drew straws to see who would get the short term. Frémont did, so he got the term that lasted only a few months.

Frémont's Last Expedition

You can follow Frémont's expedition on the map on pages 42–43.

While Frémont and his family were vacationing in Paris in 1852, he learned about another railroad **survey.** Frémont had hoped that he would be chosen to lead one of the **expeditions** the government was planning to survey various railroad routes in the West. Instead, only Army officers were selected. Frémont then decided that he would go on his own expedition anyway.

His twenty-member expedition party left in late October. Besides a **topographer** and guides, Frémont had hired an artist, Solomon Carvalho, to come along to make **daguerreotypes** of the scenery. Ten Delaware Indians also came to act as guides and to help prepare bison meat for the men.

Snow in the Rockies

The group reached the Rocky Mountains in December. The snow was very deep. They ran out of meat, and when their horses became weak and could not go on, they killed and ate them. Because they were losing horses and pack animals, they had to bury most of their equipment along the trail and come back for it. By this time, most of the men could no longer walk because their

In the 1850s, photography required much bulkier equipment than it does today. Solomon Carvalho would have had to bring chemicals, glass plates, and a heavy camera along with him.

Frémont brought Delaware Indians on his expedition because they were good hunters who knew the area. They were also good at preparing food over a campfire.

feet were frozen with **frostbite.** Their boots and moccasins were so worn out that the men ended up wrapping animal skins around their feet. One man, Oliver Fuller, died along the way.

Finally, on February 8, 1854, the group reached Parowan, a **Mormon** settlement in the Little Salt Lake Valley. The 400 residents there took the exhausted men into their homes. Most of the men stayed in Parowan for about two weeks. On February 21, Frémont and some of the men continued on through Nevada into California. As they traveled, they found a pass they thought would be excellent for a railroad. By April, Frémont was in San Francisco, but he soon returned to New York.

In Solomon Carvalho's words:

During this expedition, the men had to cross the Grand River. Carvalho compares the experience to a cabin boy clinging to the mainstay, or mast, of a ship in a storm.

"The awful plunge from the ice into the water, I never shall have the ambition to try again; the weight of my body on the horse naturally made him go under head and all; I held on as fast as a cabin boy to a main-stay in a gale of wind. If I had lost my balance it is most probable I should have been drowned. I was nearly drowned as it was, and my clothes froze stiff upon me when I came out of it."

Running for President

In 1855, the Democratic Party agreed that the popular Frémont had a good chance of winning a presidential election, and they asked him to run on their **ticket.** At the time, the country was split over whether slavery should be allowed in the new **territories** in the West. Many members of the Democratic Party thought slavery should be allowed everywhere in the country. Frémont and many others believed that it should not. When party leaders told Frémont that he could not speak out against slavery as the Democratic **candidate,** he told them that he would not run on their ticket.

Then the Republican Party approached him, asking him to be a candidate. The Republican Party had just been formed. This party was against the spread of slavery in the West. In June of 1856, the party held its **convention,** and Frémont was **nominated** as presidential candidate. Frémont immediately became the popular choice for president. In newspapers, articles were written about his adventures in the West. He was a great leader then, the newspapers said—surely he would be a great leader now.

JOHN

AND

JESSIE.

Jessie Benton Frémont was just as famous and popular as her husband. This campaign ribbon shows them both, although she herself was not a candidate.

Spreading rumors

Worried that Frémont might win, the Democratic Party began to spread stories about him. One story said that he was a secret Catholic, even though Frémont and his family worshiped regularly in the Episcopal church. (In those days, many Americans mistrusted Catholics.) Another rumor said that he was a heavy drinker, even though there was no evidence of that. The stories continued to spread. Frémont remained silent about most of the rumors. He knew they were not true and that his life would speak for itself. Still, when the election was over, Frémont lost to the Republican candidate, James Buchanan, by 536,440 votes.

For the next few years, Frémont and his family lived at their California ranch, coming back east often to stay in New York or Washington, D.C. Frémont and Jessie had five children. Two of them, Benton and Anne Beverley, died when they were infants.

Many of Frémont's opponents were in favor of slavery. This anti-Frémont ribbon tells voters that if they elect him, the slaves will be freed.

NATIVISM AND THE KNOW-NOTHING PARTY

In the 1840s many people **immigrated** to the United States from Ireland. They were poor, and nearly all of them were Catholic. In response to the large numbers of immigrants coming into the country, people began to form groups based on the idea that only people born in the United States should have the rights of full citizens. The people who believed this were called nativists. They wanted to keep foreigners out of the United States, especially foreigners who were Catholics. One nativist political party, the Know-Nothings, was growing rapidly at the time that John C. Frémont was nominated to run for President. They got their name because if members were asked about what they believed, they were told to say "I know nothing." The party lost some of its power during the Civil War because it was split over whether slavery should be outlawed. As Irish Catholics began to hold more jobs and to enter politics, the ideas behind the nativist movement became less popular. By the 1920s it had nearly disappeared.

General Frémont's Failure

In 1861, the Civil War began, with the northern states, or the Union, fighting the states in the south, called the Confederacy. Even though he had been asked to leave the army after his **court-martial,** in 1861 Frémont was named to be a general in the Union Army. He was put in charge of the Mountain Division, a large area that included Illinois and the states and **territories** between the Missouri River and the Rockies.

Frémont was sent to his headquarters in St. Louis, where he was given the task of putting together an army to protect the vast Mountain Division. He worked long hours, sometimes sleeping only four hours a night, as he tried to do his job. The Union Army, however, had little money to spare and could not give him the supplies he needed. While Frémont tried to figure out what to do, the officers under him constantly asked him for more men and more supplies. The officers complained that Frémont was not doing a good job because they could not get the supplies they needed.

Although he sometimes got into trouble with his superiors, most of the soldiers Frémont commanded were proud to have served under him.

Frémont's proclamation

Frémont learned that in Missouri, a Union state, some slaveholders were helping the Confederate Army. On August 30, 1862, Frémont declared that the slaves of anyone in Missouri who assisted the Confederates were now free. This **proclamation** made those against slavery happy. President Lincoln, however, was not happy about the proclamation. Today we often think of the Civil War as being fought over the issue of slavery.

One of Fremont's most important victories was the capture of Springfield, Missouri, from Confederate troops in 1861.

The war began, however, because states in the south were leaving the United States and forming their own government. Lincoln and others wanted to keep the Union—all the United States, including those in the south—together. They declared war on the states in the south that wanted to form their own nation. When Frémont issued his proclamation, President Lincoln was angry, saying that Frémont was making it a war about slavery instead of about preserving the Union. Lincoln gave Frémont a chance to change his mind about the proclamation, but he would not. That, along with the other complaints about Frémont, caused Lincoln to remove him from his post.

Frémont's men reacted by declaring that they would leave the army. Most of them respected their general and did not want to fight under anyone else. The people of St. Louis, who were grateful to Frémont for protecting their city, flew flags at half mast to show their sorrow. All over the country, people protested Frémont's removal.

Because Frémont was so popular, the army soon found another job for him. In March 1862, he was made head of the Mountain Department, which was made up of parts of Virginia, Tennessee, and Kentucky. Frémont stayed at that post for a while. But after a defeat against General Stonewall Jackson's Confederate forces, he became unpopular. When one of the officers who had served under him in the Mountain Division, John Pope, was named as his superior, Frémont asked to be removed from the job.

Presidential candidate again

In 1864, a group of Republicans who were unhappy with Lincoln asked Frémont to run for president. He accepted but was soon asked to step down. Having two **candidates,** he was told, was splitting the party. If he ran, Republicans would split their vote between Lincoln and Frémont. The Democratic candidate would win, and slavery would continue. Because Frémont was strongly against slavery, he withdrew from the election.

Bad investments

In 1863, Frémont joined with others to build a railroad through Kansas. He put a lot of his money into the business and trusted the wrong people.

Thomas "Stonewall" Jackson was a general in the Confederate Army during the Civil War. He got his nickname when his troops formed a strong line and refused to move at the Battle of Bull Run.

After a brilliant career and years of fame and fortune, Frémont's later years were marked by money troubles.

Because of their dishonesty and his lack of experience in business, he lost a great deal of money. He even had to give up his ranch in California. He then invested the rest of his money in another railroad deal and again lost almost all of it. He and Jessie had to sell their two homes in New York and were forced to live with friends or in small cottages.

Frémont was appointed governor of the **territory** of Arizona by President Hayes in 1878, but he was not popular with many who lived there. They did not like the fact that Frémont spent more time in New York with his family than he did in Arizona.

Writing

Jessie had always been a good writer, so to make money she began writing articles and stories for magazines. Frémont also wrote. In 1887 his **memoirs,** called *Memoirs of My Life: a Retrospective of Fifty Years,* were published. The book was expensive, though, and did not sell many copies.

In 1889 friends helped the Frémonts move to California. On July 13, 1890, while Frémont was in New York on business and away from Jessie, he suddenly got very sick and died. He was 77 years old.

Frémont's Legacy

Frémont's career as an explorer and pathmarker was very successful. The lively reports he wrote about his adventures in the West made the region come alive for many Americans who were hungry for news of the unknown regions. The maps he and his assistants made were used by the government and by travelers who went to seek their fortunes in the West. Many Americans admired Frémont's bravery and sense of adventure. He became a symbol of the American spirit and the promise of the future.

Place names

Frémont is still remembered in many places in the United States. In Frémont, Nebraska, one of the states Frémont crossed, a three-day festival is held every year in his honor. Frémont National Forest in Oregon is also named after the explorer. So are Frémont, California, and Frémont Township in Iowa.

The transcontinental railroad joined the eastern United States with the West. Its completion on May 10, 1869, was considered one of the greatest feats of the nineteenth century.

Politician

Frémont was not as successful a politician as he was an explorer. He never planned to be a politician, though. He was chosen to run for office because he was such a popular figure in America, a man who stood for freedom and bravery.

True legacy

After Frémont lost all of his money, he became sick and needed to leave New York for a sunny climate. A wealthy friend, Collis P. Huntington, paid for Frémont and Jessie to travel to California by train. When Frémont told Huntington that he should not have spent the money, Huntington replied, "You forget our road [the railroad] goes over your buried campfires and climbs many a grade you jogged over on a mule." Perhaps that was his greatest legacy—he forged the way for thousands of people, allowing them to fulfill their dreams of living in California.

In the years since Frémont led his expeditions, millions of people have settled in Los Angeles and other western cities. It would not have been possible without his efforts.

However, Frémont's **expeditions** ruined the dreams of some people. The **surveys** that he took were used by the United States government as a tool to force Native Americans off their land. They had lived on the land for hundreds, even thousands, of years, and hoped to continue living as they always had. Frémont's expeditions also opened up the West to the railroad, allowing thousands of Americans to travel West and settle there. In doing so, Native Americans were again forced to move. Eventually, the Native American tribes were given parcels of land called reservations. While even today they work to keep their ancient cultures alive, parts of their way of life have been lost forever.

Map of Frémont's Expeditions

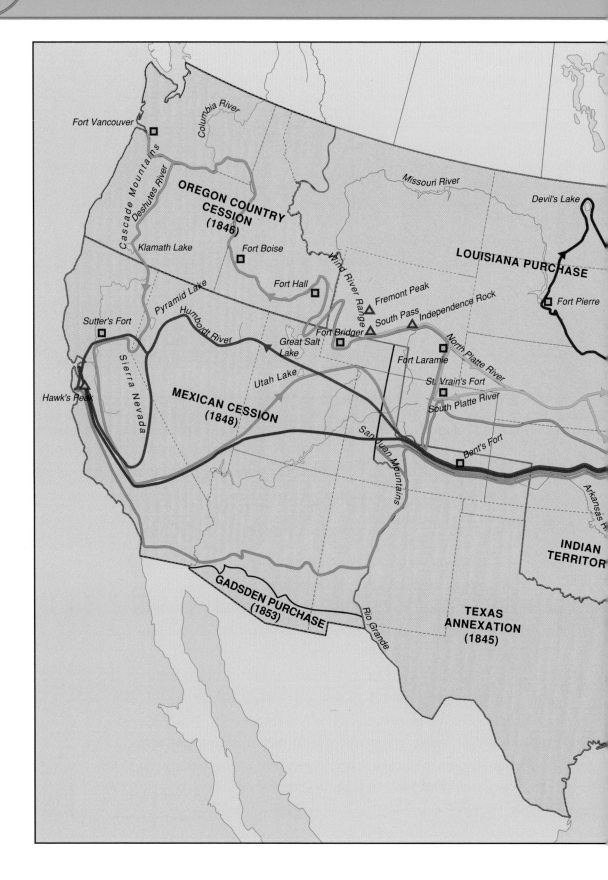

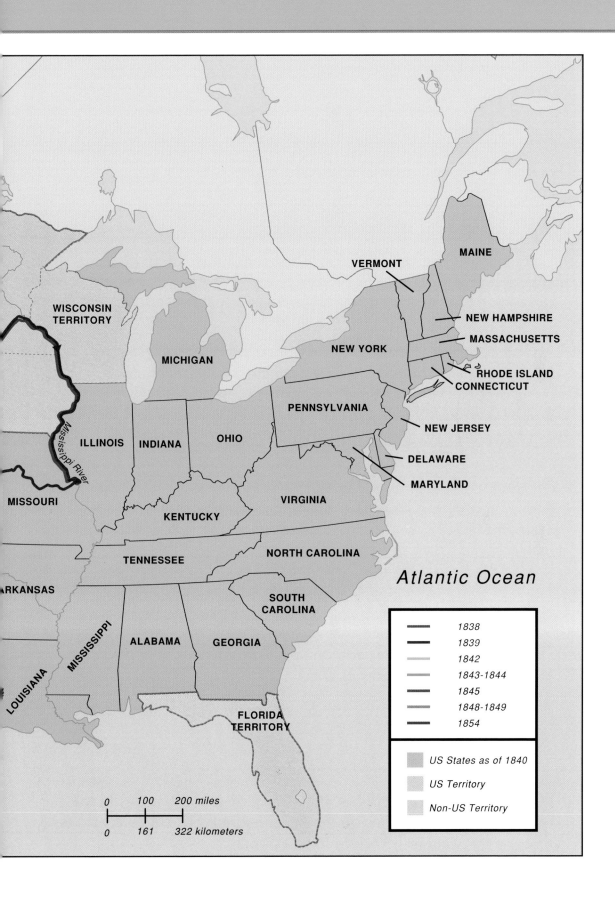

WISCONSIN
TERRITORY

MICHIGAN

Mississippi River

MISSOURI

ILLINOIS   INDIANA   OHIO

KENTUCKY

ARKANSAS

TENNESSEE

NORTH CAROLINA

MISSISSIPPI   ALABAMA   GEORGIA

SOUTH
CAROLINA

LOUISIANA

FLORIDA
TERRITORY

VERMONT   MAINE

NEW HAMPSHIRE

MASSACHUSETTS

NEW YORK

RHODE ISLAND
CONNECTICUT

PENNSYLVANIA

NEW JERSEY

DELAWARE

MARYLAND

VIRGINIA

Atlantic Ocean

———	*1838*
———	*1839*
———	*1842*
———	*1843-1844*
———	*1845*
———	*1848-1849*
———	*1854*

US States as of 1840

US Territory

Non-US Territory

0   100   200 miles

0   161   322 kilometers

Timeline

1813   On January 21, John C. Frémont is born in Savannah, Georgia.

1818   Charles Frémon dies.

1824   Jessie Ann Benton is born in Virginia on May 31.

1829   In May, Frémont enters Charleston College.

1831   On February 5, Frémont is **expelled** from Charleston College. He gets a job teaching on the *Natchez.*

1836   Frémont joins the United States **Topographical** Corps and does **surveying** work in Georgia.

1838   Frémont becomes a second **lieutenant** and goes on a surveying **expedition** with Joseph Nicolas Nicollet. The "Trail of Tears" begins.

1840   Frémont meets Thomas Hart Benton and his daughter Jessie. He and Jessie become engaged, but Frémont is sent to survey the area around the Des Moines River in Iowa

1841   Frémont and Jessie Benton **elope.**

1842   Frémont leads his first surveying expedition to the South Pass in the Rocky Mountains. On August 15, he plants a flag on the top of Frémont's Peak.

        Settlement of Oregon begins by way of the Oregon Trail.

1843–44 Frémont leads his second expedition west, passing the Great Salt Lake, the Great Basin, and the Sierra Nevada.

1845   Frémont leads a third expedition to California, where he becomes involved in a political uprising there.

1846   The United States declares war on Mexico. The Bear Flag Revolt is staged in California.

1847   Frémont is named governor of California on January 16.

1848   Frémont is **court-martialed** on January 31 and resigns from the Army. In August he leaves on his fourth expedition, surveying a pass through the southern Rockies for a railroad.

        Gold is discovered in Califonia.

1850	California becomes a state, and Frémont becomes a senator.
1853	Frémont leads his last expedition.
1856	Frémont is **nominated** as the Republican **candidate** for president but loses the election to James Buchanan.
1860	The Civil War begins, and Frémont is made a general in the Union Army.
1862	Frémont is made head of the Mountain District.
1864	Frémont is nominated again as presidential candidate, then is asked to step aside.
1865	Abraham Lincoln is assassinated on April 14.
1869	The transcontinental railroad is completed on May 10.
1878	President Rutherford B. Hayes appoints Frémont as governor of the **territory** of Arizona.
1887	Frémont's **memoirs** are published.
1890	Frémont dies in New York City on July 13.
1902	Jessie Benton Frémont dies on December 27.

More Books to Read

Carey, Charles W., Jr. *The Mexican War: Mr. Polk's War.* Berkeley Heights, N.J.: Enslow Publishers, Inc., 2002.

Faber, Harold. *John Charles Fremont: Pathfinder to the West.* Estes Park, Colo.: Benchmark Investigative Group, 2002.

Marcovitz, Hal. *John C. Fremont: Pathfinder of the West.* Broomall, Penn.: Chelsea House Publishers, 2001.

Saffer, Barbara. *The California Gold Rush.* Broomall, Penn.: Mason Crest Publishers, 2002.

Glossary

annex to add to something else, so as to become a part of it

astronomy study of the movements of stars and planets

candidate person who runs for a political office

cartographer person who makes maps

constellation group of stars in the sky that are said to make a figure or design

controversy something about which there is great difference of opinion

convention meeting of a political party at which they choose candidates and make political decisions

court-martial court that tries members of the armed forces

daguerreotype early type of photograph made on a silver plate

elope to run away to get married

expedition trip taken to discover new places

expel to force to leave

frostbite slight freezing of a part of the body

headmaster leader of a private school

immigrate to come to a foreign country to live

latitude distance north of south of the Equator

lieutenant officer in the armed forces

longitude distance east or west of the prime meridian, an imaginary line that runs through Greenwich, England

manifest destiny idea that the United States should expand all the way to the Pacific Ocean

memoirs report of a personal experience

Mormon member of the Church of Jesus Christ of Latter-day Saints, a Christian religion founded by Joseph Smith in 1830

mutiny refusal to obey authority, especially in a military situation

nominate to select to run for a political office

pioneer person who goes before and prepares the way for others to follow

proclamation official formal announcement

pueblo Native American village made up of stone or adobe houses

republic government in which supreme power lies in the citizens through their right to vote

survey to take measurements of a piece of land, using special instruments and calculating the results by means of mathematics

territory area of land under authority of a government; in the United States, not part of a state

ticket list of candidates for nomination or election to office

topographer person who uses topography to survey land with the intention of mapping it

topographical having to do with the representation of natural features on maps or charts in order to show their relative positions and sizes

tutor teacher who usually teaches a student one-on-one, outside of a regular classroom

voyageur person, almost always a man, used in the Old West and in frontier Canada to transport goods from one place to another

Index